The Romantasy Cocktail Book

52 Enchanting Recipes to Spice up Your Night

Francis Nightingale

summersdale

THE ROMANTASY COCKTAIL BOOK

Copyright © Octopus Publishing Group Limited, 2025

All rights reserved.

Text by Nicola Skinner

Illustrations by Olena Kolomiiets

No part of this book may be reproduced by any means, nor transmitted, nor translated into a machine language, without the written permission of the publishers.

Condition of Sale
This book is sold subject to the condition that it shall not, by way of trade or otherwise, be lent, resold, hired out or otherwise circulated in any form of binding or cover other than that in which it is published and without a similar condition including this condition being imposed on the subsequent purchaser.

An Hachette UK Company
www.hachette.co.uk

Summersdale Publishers
Part of Octopus Publishing Group Limited
Carmelite House
50 Victoria Embankment
LONDON
EC4Y 0DZ
UK

This FSC® label means that materials and other controlled sources used for the product have been responsibly sourced

www.summersdale.com

The authorized representative in the EEA is Hachette Ireland, 8 Castlecourt Centre, Dublin 15, D15 XTP3, Ireland (email: info@hbgi.ie)

Printed and bound in China

ISBN: 978-1-83799-730-5
eISBN: 978-1-83799-731-2

Substantial discounts on bulk quantities of Summersdale books are available to corporations, professional associations and other organizations. For details contact general enquiries: telephone: +44 (0) 1243 771107 or email: enquiries@summersdale.com.

Neither the author nor the publisher can be held responsible for any injury, loss or claim – be it health, financial or otherwise – arising out of the use, or misuse, of the suggestions made herein. Please drink responsibly.

Contents

Introduction 4

Hosting the Ultimate Romantasy Cocktail Party 5

Cocktail Kit Ideas 6

Homemade Infusions, Syrups and Bitters 7

Cocktail Glasses 8

Cocktail Terminology 10

Enchanting Cocktail Techniques 12

Liqueurs for Every Character 13

Three Guests for an Unforgettable Party 14

Tips to Break the Ice 15

Games to Play 16

DIY Decor 17

Co-Hosting Tips 18

Literary Flourishes 19

Crafting the Perfect Playlist 20

Cocktail Recipes 21

INTRODUCTION

Romantasy lovers, have you been searching to bring together some of your favourite passions? Memorable social gatherings that fit you as snugly as a beautifully cut leather corset, and enchanting cocktails that charm and seduce your senses, all blended with the sparkle of your favourite romantasy novels? Lay down your map, rest your steed and search no more. Your quest ends here.

Whether you're hosting an intimate soirée with your closest allies, planning a book club night for fellow romantasy fans or setting the stage for an evening that stretches into the early hours, the wisdom and potions inside this little book will help you achieve your heart's desire. Want tips on curating the perfect guest list? In the mood to set pulses racing? Searching for a cocktail that feels like entering a fantasy realm? Step this way, esteemed one.

With this book by your side, you'll have all the tips you need to host your festivities, and the confidence to create drinks that feel like a new chapter all of your own. So, light your candles, flick the pages. Let your story begin.

Hosting the Ultimate Romantasy Cocktail Party

Unleash hidden powers, bring together star-crossed lovers or dazzle your intended love – whatever your quest, these four tips may help you fulfil your destiny.

Spend Time on Your Invitations
Turn printed invitations into scrolls tied with ribbon or sealed with wax to create an irresistible summons to your side.

Decorate Lavishly the Night Before
Guests will be intoxicated before even taking a sip if you spend a little time on your setting. Use soft, moody lighting from candles and fairy lights, and velvet cushions and vintage decor that will transport guests to an otherworldly haven – where anything is possible.

Provide Spellbinding Garnishes
Set up a dedicated bar with fresh herbs, edible flowers and shimmering dust to let guests personalize drinks with their own love spells and deepest wishes.

Conjure Tokens of Magic
Send guests home with tiny vials of bitters or liqueur as a lasting memento of your enchanted evening. Embellish them with dried herbs or your favourite romantasy quotes.

Cocktail Kit Ideas

Master the art of homemade heavenly elixirs with these five must-haves for every master or mistress of ceremony. Each will bring a touch of allure to your gathering.

- **Crystal decanters and bottles** – so you can display spirits in glass vessels that glow like relics under candlelight.

- **A lemon zester** – to add delicate citrus zest curls to cocktails for a fragrant, delicate flair.

- **A muddler** – helps you crush herbs, berries and spices to release enchanting aromas and flavours, giving your drinks depth, twists and surprises.

- **A fine mesh strainer** – helps you achieve a smooth finish by straining out bits of herbs or pulp, ensuring each drink is as refined as it is magical.

- **A cocktail shaker** – a stylish accessory to help you blend your potions to perfection. When you're in the mood to captivate or conquer, the combination of crashing ice and flashing metal will shake – and stir – all the senses alive.

Homemade Infusions, Syrups and Bitters

Whether you want to dazzle your potential soulmate or protect a loved one, these essences will bring the potency of legends past to your cocktails. Conserve your energy for the night in question by making these in advance.

Lavender Love Syrup

Combine equal parts sugar and water, adding one or two sprigs of fresh or dried lavender. Simmer until aromatic, then strain. Associated with calm and love, lavender adds a perfect touch of romantic enchantment to gin or champagne.

Protective Shield Gin

Infuse fresh rosemary sprigs in a bottle of gin for three days. This "herb of remembrance" is believed to improve memory and ward off evil, and the infusion brings an earthy, protective aura to martinis or gin and tonics.

Healing Honey Tint

Blend 2 tablespoons of honey with 1 litre of warm water and half a teaspoon of crushed cardamom pods, steep overnight, and strain. Cardamom has been revered since Ancient Egyptian times, and is associated with healing and protection. This syrup lends warmth and wisdom to whisky cocktails.

Cocktail Glasses

Whether you're charming a soulmate, celebrating with fellow adventurers or savouring a magical night, if you want to truly dazzle, have the right glass for the right drink.

Coupe

For glamorous champagne cocktails or dainty sips, this elegant bowl is ideal for shaken drinks.

Flute

Ideal for celebrations, the flute captures the effervescence of champagne and prosecco, turning every toast into a mythical moment.

Gin Balloon

A beautiful glass bowl on a stem, great for serving anything with a bright or herbal character.

Highball

A must-have for tall, refreshing potions like Forbidden Nectar (p.65) or New Beginnings (p.125). Its sleek form is perfect for soda-topped spirits.

Hurricane
This stormy-shaped glass is ideal for tropical concoctions like the Frosted Fruit Fable (p.117), making every sip feel sun-kissed and exotic.

Long Shot
The go-to for potent shooters and layered mini-cocktails – each sip a quick, fiery spell.

Margarita
Shaped like a blooming flower, this glass is perfect for salt-rimmed, flavour-packed margaritas.

Martini
The classic choice for drinks where elegance meets intrigue, like a Sundown Serenade (p.37) or a Dreamspinner (p.109).

Old-Fashioned
Sturdy and timeless, perfect for spirit-forward cocktails such as Starlight Spritz (p.23).

Cocktail Terminology

New to the world of cocktails? Fear not, adventurer! You too can speak the language of the mixologist, and mix, shake and stir with confidence.

Neat
Pure spirit served straight up, no ice – think of it as the drink's unfiltered essence.

On the Rocks
A neat measure, but poured over ice cubes, cooling the drink without diluting its character too much.

Shaken
A technique that blends ingredients (usually with ice) in a cocktail shaker for a chilled, frothy effect.

Stirred
Gentler than shaking, this method mixes spirits with a bar spoon to keep them silky smooth.

Muddled
Crushing herbs, fruits or spices with a muddler to release their flavours.

Twist
A citrus peel garnish, twisted to release fragrant oils – adds flair and aroma to any drink.

Bitters
Concentrated flavour extracts that add depth and complexity, transforming your cocktail into a potion of intrigue.

Dry
Refers to a cocktail with less sweetness – often achieved by using dry vermouth in martinis.

Up
Served chilled in a stemmed glass, without ice.

Enchanting Cocktail Techniques

Mastering these cocktail-making methods will help you wield great power – and look pretty cool, too.

The Spellbinding Shake
Combine your ingredients with ice in a cocktail shaker and shake vigorously. This method chills your potion while infusing it with tiny air bubbles, creating a frothy, bewitching texture.

The Silken Stir
For a smoother, more elegant potion, stirring is the key. Combine spirits with ice in a mixing glass and stir gently with a bar spoon. This technique preserves clarity, making it ideal for sophisticated sippers.

The Mystical Muddle
Unleash the hidden powers of fresh herbs, fruits or spices by muddling them in your glass. This method releases essential oils and juices, adding a burst of flavour to your drinks.

The Captivating Layer
For those looking to dazzle, try layering your ingredients. Gently pour spirits over the back of a spoon into a glass to create beautiful, colourful striations – a true potion for the eyes.

Liqueurs for Every Character

Whether you're crafting a drink for fate-bound lovers or a potion for an irresistible rake, here are liqueur ideas for your favourite archetypes.

The Star-Crossed Lover – Amaretto
Sweet, bittersweet and almond-rich, amaretto captures the heartbreak and passion of ill-fated romance. Perfect for those who love against all odds.

The Enigmatic Rogue – Spiced Rum
Bold and full of secrets, spiced rum channels the charm of a dashing rogue who's lived a thousand adventures. Ideal for dark and stormy moments.

The Mystic Seer – Elderflower Liqueur
Floral and ethereal, elderflower brings the wisdom of a clairvoyant. Add a splash to gin or champagne for a cocktail that feels like a prophecy.

The Noble Warrior – Whisky
Strong and full-bodied, whisky embodies the courage of a loyal knight. Best served in an Old-Fashioned to honour valour.

The Enchanted Fae – Absinthe
Mysterious and a bit dangerous, absinthe captures the allure of the fae. Suited to a mystical-looking cocktail that dances between worlds.

Three Guests for an Unforgettable Party

A cocktail soirée isn't just about the drinks you serve, but also the enchanting souls who sip them. Here are three guests who shouldn't be left off the list.

The Charismatic Storyteller

Every party needs a bard – someone whose tales captivate every ear and break the ice fast. If you have any acquaintance who can turn even a trip to the supermarket into a captivating story, that's your storyteller.

The Mischievous Flirt

This guest knows how to keep things playful with a wink, a sly grin and a talent for making every moment feel charged with a little extra spark. Watch as they turn the quiet corners into places of whispered secrets. Know someone who's never short of admirers? That's your flirt.

The Dancefloor Enchanter

Whether it's an impromptu waltz or a full-on dance battle, this guest gets everyone moving. Their energy is infectious, transforming your living room into a dance hall, ensuring no one leaves without a few twirls and dips.

Tips to Break the Ice

For a night that feels plucked from the pages of a romantasy novel, set the stage with these enchanting, flirty touches.

- **Welcome with a potion of intrigue** – Greet guests with drinks that feel like magic – sparkling mocktails or herbal elixirs – and enlist a "knight-at-arms" to stand at the door, ensuring no one begins their quest without this spellbinding start.

- **Spark fated connections** – Scatter conversation starters near the entrance: cards asking, "What's your favourite slow-burn love story?" or "Enemies-to-lovers – yes or no?" These playful prompts create fateful moments with shared smiles and glances.

- **Be the charismatic ruler** – As host, you're the sovereign of this magical realm, gliding gracefully through your court. Offer compliments as warm as a knight's embrace and ask questions that uncover hidden truths, making everyone feel they've danced in moonlight.

- **Weave in playful quests** – Plan games like treasure hunts, secret missions or audacious dares. These adventures spark laughter, build alliances and ensure even the quietest soul has their moment to shine.

Games to Play

Whether you seek to uncover hidden truths, bond over adventures or test your guests' wit in a world of magic, these games will turn your cocktail party into the stuff of legend in your circles.

The Enchanted Tarot Challenge

Each guest draws a tarot card and must craft a short story or prophecy based on their card. This game is sure to bring out your guests' special talents – and break the ice through the magic of storytelling.

Fabled Creature Charades

Guests act out famous romantasy creatures – like a dragon, fae or vampire – without speaking. The rest must guess who they are. This playful game sparks laughter and ignites imagination, with the winner choosing a special cocktail.

Spellbinding Wordsmiths

Pass around random words like "moonlit", "whispers" or "ancient curse". Each guest must create a short, impromptu romantic or adventurous tale. This game stirs creativity, turning your evening into a vibrant narrative.

DIY Decor

Turn any space into an enchanting realm with budget-friendly touches for a magical, fantastical vibe.

- 🌹 **Twinkling fairy lights** – Drape warm fairy lights around windows, mirrors or walls to create a starry glow. These simple lights transform any room into a magical twilight haven.

- 🌹 **Mystical candles** – Scatter mismatched candles – real or battery-powered – throughout your space. Their flickering light adds ethereal ambience, turning mundane clutter into spellbinding decor.

- 🌹 **DIY potion bottles** – Repurpose old glass bottles into "potion bottles". Fill them with coloured water, glitter or herbs, and display them on tables or shelves for an alchemist's den vibe.

- 🌹 **Velvet throws and pillows** – Add affordable luxury with plush velvet throws and pillows in rich tones like emerald or burgundy. These touches evoke royalty and warmth.

Co-Hosting Tips

Why host alone when friends can share the fun? Dividing duties ensures an enchanting, stress-free evening. Here are three essential co-hosting roles to keep your party running smoothly.

The Potion Master
Appoint a friend as "potion master" to craft signature cocktails and mix classics, ensuring a steady flow of drinks. Bonus points if they don a wizard's robe for flair!

The Gatekeeper of Garnishes
Assign someone to manage the garnish station. From rosemary sprigs to citrus twists, garnishes are replenished and drinks stay as enchanting as they taste with someone in this role.

The Storyteller
Enlist a storyteller to keep the energy alive. This person introduces guests, sparks conversation and sets a whimsical tone by leading a themed game or offering a magical toast.

By sharing responsibilities, your gathering feels like a beautifully orchestrated court dance, leaving everyone – especially you – free to enjoy the night and the adventures that you create.

Literary Flourishes

Transport your guests into the worlds of your favourite romantasy novels with imaginative touches that turn your cocktail party into a living storybook.

Character-Inspired Cocktails

Base your drinks on beloved characters or iconic moments from favourite novels. Use ingredients that reflect their essence – herbal notes for a witch, sparkling finishes for a celestial being. Illustrate characters with matching cocktails and display them above your bar for a personal touch.

Literary Decor

Infuse your space with decor that reflects your cherished stories. Drape velvet curtains, scatter old books as centrepieces and frame cherished quotes for display. Create a "storybook corner" where guests can browse novels, adding an interactive and magical element.

Themed Activities

Plan a quick themed game tied to your favourite book worlds. Try a "Wand Crafting Challenge" or a "Choose Your Fates" card game to keep guests immersed in the fantasy, sparking laughter and lasting memories.

With these touches, your cocktail party becomes a journey through the fantastical worlds you hold dear.

Crafting the Perfect Playlist

The right music sets a tone that's both electric and enchanting. Here's how to create a dynamic, romantasy-inspired soundtrack:

- 🌹 **Start with a captivating intro** – Open the night with ambient tunes that whisper intrigue and allure – soft, mystical melodies or sultry ballads to draw guests into your world.

- 🌹 **Create a collaborative playlist** – Invite your guests to co-create the magic by contributing to a shared playlist. Ask them to add songs that embody their idea of forbidden love, daring adventure or celestial passion.

- 🌹 **Rotate DJ duty** – Hand the reins to your guests for a song or two. Each new player adds a spark of mystery or passion, keeping the atmosphere alive with unexpected twists.

- 🌹 **Match music to moments** – Curate the soundtrack for specific scenes of your night. Pair dark, sensual tracks with the clink of cocktail glasses, and choose ethereal, high-energy tunes during games or laughter-filled conversations.

Cocktail Recipes

Imbibe the light of the stars with this dazzling cocktail. Bright and bold, this celestial sip bestows the drinker with the brilliance of the heavens – perfect for a party or for marking any joyful celebration.

Ingredients

- 3 sprigs of thyme, plus some for a garnish
- 60 ml (2 fl oz) gin
- 30 ml (1 fl oz) limoncello
- 30 ml (1 fl oz) lime juice, freshly squeezed
- Ice cubes, for shaker and glass
- Soda water, to top
- Lemon slices, to garnish

Method

Muddle two sprigs of thyme in the cocktail shaker, then add the ice.

Pour in the gin, limoncello and lime juice and shake thoroughly.

Strain into a glass and top with soda water. Add more ice cubes if desired.

Garnish with one sprig of thyme and lemon slices.

Give in to temptation with this sweet-but-sharp cocktail, which fizzes on your tongue and leaves you wanting more. This is a recipe with which to romance your beloved or seduce your enemies – the choice is yours…

Ingredients

- 15 ml (½ fl oz) crème de cassis
- Champagne, chilled, to top
- Frozen blackberries, to garnish

Method

Add the crème de cassis to the flute.

Top with champagne.

Garnish with frozen blackberries.

Fire's Lick

Ignite something special with Fire's Lick, a bold elixir for the brave and passionate. Spicy and intense, this potion will embolden the heart and warm the mouth with flickering heat – ideal for fiery gatherings, hot court news or thrilling rendezvous.

Ingredients

- 50 ml (1⅔ fl oz) vodka
- 240 ml (8 fl oz) tomato juice
- 15 ml (½ fl oz) lemon juice
- Ice cubes
- 8 dashes hot pepper sauce
- 8 dashes Worcestershire sauce
- Pinch celery salt
- Pinch black pepper
- Celery stalk, to serve

Method

Combine the ice and all the ingredients except the celery stalk in a cocktail shaker.

Shake firmly and strain into a highball glass.

Garnish with stick of celery.

Orchard Flame

Seduce them to their very core with a drink as innocent as an orchard stroll – until the heat kicks in. Bold, fiery and seductively smooth, this potion tempts the senses with a veneer of wholesome goodness.

Ingredients

- 60 ml (2 fl oz) cinnamon whisky liqueur
- 60 ml (2 fl oz) vanilla vodka
- 120 ml (4 fl oz) cloudy apple juice
- Sliced, dried apple, to serve

Method

Combine the whisky and vodka directly in the glass.

Gently heat the apple juice in a saucepan until warmed through and pour over the alcohol.

Garnish with sliced apple.

True gems will savour the power of amethyst with each sweet, floral sip of this beautiful drink. The violet hues whisper ancient wisdom, an invitation to heed the quiet voices of oracles and their powerful crystals.

Ingredients

- 60 ml (2 fl oz) gin
- 15 ml (½ fl oz) lemon juice
- 15 ml (½ fl oz) maraschino liqueur
- 15 ml (½ fl oz) crème de violette
- Ice cubes
- Lemon peel and cherries, to garnish

Method

Add the ice and all the ingredients except the garnish to a cocktail shaker.

Shake until combined and cooled.

Strain into a coupe glass.

Garnish with twisted lemon peel and cherries.

Sweet Betrayal

A drink that catches you off-guard, as irresistible as a forbidden kiss. Its butter-wouldn't-melt taste hides a fiery kick that leaves you wanting more – an enchanting, unexpected treat for pleasure-seekers who dare to indulge.

Ingredients

- 30 ml (1 fl oz) coffee liqueur
- 30 ml (1 fl oz) Irish cream liqueur
- 30 ml (1 fl oz) vodka
- 60 ml (2 fl oz) milk or heavy cream
- Ice cubes
- 1 tsp chocolate sauce (from a squeezy bottle), to garnish
- Chocolate chips, to garnish

Method

Add all the ingredients, apart from the garnishes and ice, to the cocktail shaker. Shake until combined.

Add ice to the cocktail shaker and shake well until chilled.

Squirt chocolate sauce up the inside of the glass for decoration.

Strain the cocktail into the glass.

Top with chocolate chips to garnish.

WE SCARLET THREE

A potent trio, so perfectly chilled and elegantly served you'd never guess how dangerously delicious they are. Beauty, elegance and heat – a true triple threat.

Ingredients

- 60 ml (2 fl oz) brandy
- 60 ml (2 fl oz) cognac
- 60 ml (2 fl oz) sweet vermouth
- Ice cubes

Method

Stir together all ingredients in a cocktail shaker until well chilled.

Strain into the martini glass.

Celebrate the promise of unspoken adventures still to come with this sultry tribute to the pink-drenched hues of the day's end. Mark the line between day and night – for those who like to step between shadow and light.

Ingredients

- 30 ml (1 fl oz) vodka
- 30 ml (1 fl oz) triple sec
- 90 ml (3 fl oz) cranberry juice
- 30 ml (1 fl oz) lime juice
- Ice cubes
- Twist of lime, to garnish

Method

Add all of the ingredients, except for the garnish, to a cocktail shaker.

Shake until everything is combined and chilled.

Strain into a martini glass and add a twist of lime to garnish.

HEART'S TEMPEST

Like lovers entwined in the heart of an ice storm, this cocktail is intense, exhilarating and laced with the bittersweet tang of tempest-flung passion. Be prepared for the rage of the heavens – and the intoxicating beauty within.

Ingredients

- 20 ml (⅔ fl oz) vodka
- 20 ml (⅔ fl oz) amaro
- Splash of limoncello
- 40 ml (1⅓ fl oz) orange juice
- 40 ml (1⅓ fl oz) apple and raspberry juice
- Ice cubes, for shaker and glass
- Bitter lemon, to top
- Sprig of mint, to garnish

Method

Add all of the ingredients, expect the bitter lemon and mint, to a cocktail shaker.

Shake until combined and chilled.

Strain into an ice-filled highball glass.

Top with bitter lemon and garnish with mint.

Sip of the Sage

If you need answers, take refuge in this elixir of quiet wisdom, a drink that unfolds in layers, inviting introspection and calm. Feel it unleash clarity, warmth and the gentle comfort of age-old truths.

Ingredients

- 1 lemon, cut into 4 wedges
- 4 mint leaves, plus a sprig to garnish
- 60 ml (2 fl oz) bourbon
- 15 ml (½ fl oz) simple or maple syrup
- Ice cubes, for shaker and glass

Method

First muddle the lemon wedges in a cocktail shaker (without ice) until the juices have released.

Then add the mint and muddle until bruised.

Add ice and the remaining ingredients, except for the garnish, shaking well to combine before straining into an ice-filled glass.

Simple syrup and maple syrup work equally well – pick simple syrup if you have a sweet tooth and maple if you prefer a slightly more complicated flavour profile.

Garnish with sprig of mint.

Pure Allure

Charisma in a glass, this is where simplicity meets sensuality in every sip. Effortlessly chic and refreshingly bold, it beckons with quiet seduction, leaving a lingering taste of desire that enchants everyone who dares to indulge.

Ingredients

- 60 ml (2 fl oz) white rum
- 20 ml (⅔ fl oz) lime juice
- 15 ml (½ fl oz) simple syrup
- Ice cubes
- Lime wheel, to garnish

Method

Shake together the liquid ingredients and ice in a cocktail shaker.

Strain into the glass when chilled and garnish with lime wheel.

Amber Alchemy

Wizards and spell weavers will savour the artistry of this radiant creation, born of patience and skill. Each taste reveals the harmony of craft and care, a golden testament to the transformative magic of true mastery.

Ingredients

- 40 ml (1⅓ fl oz) dry vermouth
- 40 ml (1⅓ fl oz) sweet vermouth
- 1 dash maraschino liqueur
- 2 dashes Angostura bitters
- Ice cubes
- Twist of orange peel, to garnish

Method

Add all the ingredients, except the garnish, to a cocktail shaker.

Gently stir the mixture. Do not shake – shaking the mixture can froth and cloud the vermouth and this cocktail looks most inviting in its original clear amber.

Strain into a martini glass and garnish with twist of orange peel.

Lagoon Plunge

Immerse yourself in a luminous blend that captures the allure of virgin waters – and the adventures that can be found beneath the seemingly calm surface. How deep will you go, and what treasure will you discover?

Ingredients

- 30 ml (1 fl oz) vodka
- 30 ml (1 fl oz) blue curaçao
- Ice cubes
- 120 ml (4 fl oz) lemonade
- Lemon peel, to garnish

Method

Combine the vodka and blue curaçao in an ice-filled glass and stir until well chilled.

Top with lemonade and gently stir to combine.

Garnish with lemon.

Playful and irresistible, this dances on the tongue like laughter shared in a secret garden, bathed in golden light. Bright, bubbly and just a little naughty, it's the perfect prelude to sun-kissed seduction.

Ingredients

- 60 ml (2 fl oz) Aperol
- 120 ml (4 fl oz) prosecco
- Ice cubes
- Soda water, to top

Method

Add several whole ice cubes to the glass.

Pour in the Aperol and prosecco and stir together.

Top with the soda water.

Snow Queen's Shadows

Savour the darker side of the Snow Queen's realm and the dazzling allure of her ice-cold beauty, where shadows linger. One thing's for sure – with this potion in your hand, there'll be a delicious storm cloud in every sip.

Ingredients

- 1 overripe banana
- 60 ml (2 fl oz) white rum
- 30 ml (1 fl oz) coffee liqueur
- 30 ml (1 fl oz) crème de banana
- 30 ml (1 fl oz) crème de cacao (optional)
- 60 ml (2 fl oz) single cream or coconut cream
- Crushed ice

Method

Peel the banana and break into chunks. Optional – before you do this, slice off tip with peel on and retain for a garnish.

Blend the banana and all of the remaining ingredients with crushed ice.

Pour into a glass.

For some drama, hold back the coffee liqueur and pour over cocktail once transferred to glass. This will filter down in dark rolling clouds.

Kingdom Crasher

Let the rule-breaking begin with this fierce, bold, unapologetic brew. The flavours strike like a sudden storm, shaking foundations and leaving a trail of unforgettable energy in their wake. Drink if you dare, and prepare for the realm to tremble.

Ingredients

- 60 ml (2 fl oz) tequila
- 20 ml (⅔ fl oz) crème de cassis
- 60 ml (2 fl oz) lime juice
- Ice cubes, for shaker and glass
- Ginger beer, to top
- Lime quarter, to garnish

Method

Add all of the ingredients, except for the ginger beer and garnish, to a cocktail shaker.

Shake the mixture until fully combined and chilled.

Strain into an ice-filled glass.

Gently top with ginger beer and garnish with lime quarter.

Like a long-dormant empire stirring to life, this drink is a tribute to timeless tastes, power and passion. Bold and undeniable, it marches on our tongue to announce its renaissance.

Ingredients

- 70 ml (2⅖ fl oz) whisky (rye or bourbon)
- 35 ml (1⅕ fl oz) sweet vermouth
- 2–3 dashes aromatic bitters
- Ice cubes
- 1 cherry or small slice of lemon peel

Method

Pour the whisky (rye is recommended but bourbon is fine if preferred), vermouth and bitters into the ice-filled shaker.

Stir lightly and carefully, but well. Shaking will make the cocktail cloudy to the eye and oily to the taste.

Strain the drink into the martini glass and garnish with the lemon peel or cherry.

Fresh Craving

There's nothing as intoxicating as a brand-new crush. This little tincture mirrors the electric thrill of a fledgling infatuation – fresh, vibrant and brimming with possibility. Each drop is a spark, the beginning of something exciting and yet to be discovered.

Ingredients

- 60 ml (2 fl oz) gin
- 75 ml (2½ fl oz) cloudy apple juice
- 30 ml (1 fl oz) elderflower cordial
- 30 ml (1 fl oz) lime juice, freshly squeezed
- Ice cubes, for shaker and glass
- Handful of mint leaves, to garnish
- Cucumber wheel, to garnish

Method

Add the ingredients, except for the garnish, to the cocktail shaker.

Shake until combined and chilled.

Strain into an ice-filled glass.

Garnish with mint leaves and cucumber.

Ignite the senses with a passionate, unforgettable connection that's as sharp and intoxicating as a first touch. Whether you need to rouse yourself for conquest, battle or love, this will get you up and start you right.

Ingredients

- 60 ml (2 fl oz) vodka
- 30 ml (1 fl oz) espresso coffee, cooled
- 15 ml (½ fl oz) coffee liqueur
- 15 ml (½ fl oz) simple syrup
- Ice cubes
- Coffee beans, to garnish
- Chocolate shavings, to garnish (optional)

Method

Add all the ingredients, except for the garnishes, to a cocktail shaker.

Shake until combined and chilled.

Strain into martini glass.

Float coffee beans on top for a finishing flourish. Sprinkle chocolate shavings over the serving if you have a sweet tooth.

Power's Whisper

Simple, classic, captivating. This beautifully understated blend is crisp and effervescent and knows its worth – perfect for the one who commands attention without trying.

Ingredients

- 60 ml (2 fl oz) gin
- 30 ml (1 fl oz) lemon juice
- 15 ml (½ fl oz) simple syrup
- Ice cubes
- Champagne, to top
- Lemon peel twist, to garnish

Method

Add the gin, lemon juice, simple syrup and ice to a cocktail shaker. Shake until combined and chilled.

Strain into a champagne flute.

Top with champagne.

Garnish with lemon peel.

Sleigh Ride to Midnight

As snowflakes kiss the air and the world blurs into a moon-kissed dream, embark on a midnight rendezvous that promises warmth, desire and the spice of secret meetings across the ice.

Ingredients

- 1 whole egg (pasteurized)
- 60 ml (2 fl oz) gin
- 15 ml (½ fl oz) simple syrup
- Ice cubes
- Grated nutmeg, to garnish

Method

Shake the egg, gin, simple syrup and ice together in a cocktail shaker.

Strain into a glass, empty the shaker of ice and return mixture to shaker.

Shake a second time and strain into martini glass.

Dust with grated nutmeg to garnish.

Forbidden Nectar

If you've got your sights set on a forbidden love, this cocktail brings just the right warmth, depth and a teasing dash of vitality to give you the courage to cross that line – and to hell with the consequences.

Ingredients

- 90 ml (3 fl oz) dark rum
- 15 ml (½ fl oz) simple syrup
- 25 ml (⅘ fl oz) lemon or lime juice
- 10 ml (⅓ fl oz) grenadine
- 2 dashes Angostura bitters
- Ice cubes, for shaker and glass
- Soda water, to top
- Pinch grated nutmeg, to garnish
- Sprig of mint, to garnish

Method

Add all ingredients, except the soda and garnishes, to the cocktail shaker.

Shake vigorously to create the frothy top.

Strain into an ice-filled glass.

Top with soda water.

Sprinkle a pinch of nutmeg and garnish with a sprig of mint.

Enjoy the ease of a dreamlike drink that slips down effortlessly, embodying ivory silk and beautifully dressed soirées with its frothy, light allure. Flirtatious and enchanting, it's the perfect blend of elegance and delight. How quickly will your stocking go down?

Ingredients

- 60 ml (2 fl oz) gin
- 15 ml (½ fl oz) lemon juice
- 15 ml (½ fl oz) lime juice
- 15 ml (½ fl oz) simple syrup
- 15 ml (½ fl oz) cream
- 1 egg white (pasteurized)
- 3 dashes orange blossom water
- Ice cubes
- Soda water, to top

Method

Add all of the ingredients, except the soda, to a cocktail shaker.

Shake until very frothy – this can take up to 5 minutes!

Strain into a glass.

Top with soda water and enjoy.

This is a drink of hidden paradises, where the air is rich with secrets and the sweetness of forbidden fruit. Beneath its gilded allure lies a depth that tempts, teases and lingers.

Ingredients

- 30 ml (1 fl oz) gin
- 30 ml (1 fl oz) cherry brandy
- 30 ml (1 fl oz) herbal liqueur, such as Bénédictine
- 1 dash Angostura bitters
- Ice cubes, for shaker and glass
- 60 ml (2 fl oz) pineapple juice
- 30 ml (1 fl oz) lime juice
- Sparkling water, to top
- Maraschino cherry, to garnish
- Orange slice, to garnish

Method

Add the gin, cherry brandy, herbal liqueur, Angostura bitters and ice to a cocktail shaker.

Stir until chilled and combined.

Pour into an ice-filled glass and stir in pineapple juice and lime juice.

Top with sparkling water. Garnish with cherry and orange slice.

Sunfire Bloom

As dawn stretches its golden fingers across the sky, hearts awaken to new promises. With every drop, feel the warmth of bonds being forged – of friendships blossoming and lovers pledging loyalty, as bright and hopeful as the sun's first light.

Ingredients

- 15 ml (½ fl oz) grenadine
- 60 ml (2 fl oz) silver tequila
- 120 ml (4 fl oz) orange juice
- Ice cubes, for shaker and glass
- Orange slice, to garnish

Method

Pour the grenadine into the bottom of an ice-filled glass.

Shake tequila and orange juice in a cocktail shaker filled with ice until chilled and combined.

Pour mixture into the glass carefully.

Garnish with orange slice.

Stolen Moment

When intrigue, passion and drama run high, every hero and heroine deserves a refreshing sip to quench their thirst before diving back into the heart of the fervour. This drink is that moment. Take it before plunging back into the fray – or play.

Ingredients

- 60 ml (2 fl oz) peach schnapps
- 140 ml (4⅔ fl oz) orange juice
- Ice cubes, for shaker and glass
- Orange slices, to garnish

Method

Add schnapps, orange juice and ice to a cocktail shaker.

Shake until combined and chilled.

Strain into a glass.

Add slices of orange and ice cubes if desired.

Some elixirs are simply impossible to resist – as are their drinkers. Eternally beautiful to behold, and delicious to imbibe, you must approach this cocktail carefully – for once in hand, your allure will become an irresistible force.

Ingredients

- 60 ml (2 fl oz) gin
- 30 ml (1 fl oz) lime juice
- 15 ml (½ fl oz) simple syrup
- Ice cubes
- Lime slice, to garnish

Method

Shake the gin, lime juice and simple syrup in a cocktail shaker filled with ice until chilled.

Strain into the martini glass.

Garnish with slice of lime.

Stormbound Pledge

Rising tall and untamed, dive into layered depths reflecting promises that come from the heart. Each sip carries the thrill of whispered vows beneath storm-laden skies – a drink for those who embrace the tempest within.

Ingredients

- 120 ml (4 fl oz) chilled ginger beer
- 30 ml (1 fl oz) lime juice
- Ice cubes
- 60 ml (2 fl oz) dark or spiced rum
- Lime wedge, to garnish

Method

Add the ginger beer and lime juice to an ice-filled glass and gently stir.

Pour over the rum to create a dramatic layered effect.

Garnish with a wedge of lime.

The flavours also work well when combined, so, if preferred, add first the rum and lime juice, then the ginger beer and gently stir.

Ruby by the Firelight

Gleaming like a precious gem in the firelight, this beautiful little drink will enchant hearts – and eyes – with its vibrant allure. Each nip brims with sparkle and beauty, and is perfect for those who want to dazzle an intended.

Ingredients

- 60 ml (2 fl oz) gin
- 15 ml (½ fl oz) triple sec
- 15 ml (½ fl oz) grenadine
- 20 ml (⅔ fl oz) lemon juice
- Ice cubes, for shaker and glass
- Soda water, to top

Method

Add all the ingredients, except the soda water, to a cocktail shaker.

Shake until combined and cool.

Strain into an ice-filled glass and top with soda water.

A silken promise where the refined elegance of court meets the fiery kick of a rebellious outsider. Dive into a deep, creamy sweetness that lingers like shared secrets, stolen glances and adventures to come under candlelight.

Ingredients

- 60 ml (2 fl oz) bourbon
- 20 ml (⅔ fl oz) lemon juice
- 15 ml (½ fl oz) simple syrup
- 15 ml (½ fl oz) egg white (pasteurized)
- Ice cubes
- Orange twist and a maraschino cherry, to garnish

Method

Add ingredients (without ice or garnish) to a cocktail shaker.

Shake with gusto until the mixture is frothy.

Add ice and shake again until chilled.

Strain into a coupe glass. If successful, a thin layer of white froth should top the cocktail.

For an added touch, garnish with orange twist and a maraschino cherry.

Heart of the Green Flame

An evergreen heart that always burns with wild intensity, this is where sweetness and sharpness entwine in an endless embrace. If you crackle with passion and seek a drink that mirrors the rich desire in your heart, this will satisfy your craving, even if fate does not.

Ingredients

- 1 lime, cut into wedges
- 2 tsp white caster sugar
- 60 ml (2 fl oz) cachaça
- Ice cubes
- Lime slices, to garnish

Method

Add all ingredients to the glass and muddle together vigorously, until you're sure the lime has released its juice and the sugar is dissolved.

Fill the glass with ice and stir.

Garnish with lime slices.

Firelight Fling

Let's draw a little closer to the seductive crackle of the hearth with a suitable companion who is stoking the spark between you. Here's a fleeting moment of heat and light, where passion flickers, flares and burns magnificently, and nothing is left untouched.

Ingredients

- 60 ml (2 fl oz) whisky
- 1 tbsp white caster sugar
- Ice cubes
- 1 orange, quartered, plus two slices to garnish

Method

Muddle the whisky, sugar and orange quarters in a cocktail shaker.

Strain the mixture into an ice-filled glass and garnish with two slices of orange.

Trailblazer's Elixir

Celebrate difference with this potion that brings to mind daring adventurers and enterprising innovators, whose passion for new experiences changes reigns and moves mountains. If you seek to take the road less travelled, this one's got your name on it.

Ingredients

- 1 kiwi, with peel removed
- 60 ml (2 fl oz) vodka
- 45 ml (1½ fl oz) lemon juice
- 15 ml (½ fl oz) simple syrup
- Ice cubes, for shaker and glass
- Soda water, to top
- Kiwi slice, to garnish

Method

Muddle the kiwi in the base of a cocktail shaker. Then add ice, vodka, lemon juice and simple syrup and shake vigorously until combined.

Strain into an ice-filled glass and top with soda water.

Garnish with slice of kiwi.

Peaks of Desire

Rising like the dawn over jagged crags of ice, true desire knows no limits or barriers. Let the warmth of daybreak and the exhilaration of the climb tease the senses, igniting passion as the mountain's promise of exhilaration unfolds.

Ingredients

- 60 ml (2 fl oz) gin
- 30 ml (1 fl oz) lemon juice
- 15 ml (½ fl oz) simple syrup
- Ice cubes, for shaker and glass
- 15 ml (½ fl oz) crème de mûre
- Blackberries or lemon slice, to garnish

Method

Add the gin, lemon juice, simple syrup and ice to a cocktail shaker.

Shake well until chilled and combined.

Strain into an ice-filled glass. Pour the crème de mûre on top of the cocktail to create a dramatic ombre effect.

Garnish with blackberries or, if not available, lemon slice.

Princess in Waiting

All eyes are on this delicate, berry-infused elixir, sweet yet full of potential. Like a new maiden princess poised for greatness, it's an alluring drink that hints at the power she's destined to command.

Ingredients

- 60 ml (2 fl oz) gold rum
- 15 ml (½ fl oz) orange curaçao
- 15 ml (½ fl oz) lime juice
- 15 ml (½ fl oz) raspberry syrup
- Ice cubes, for shaker and glass
- Fresh raspberries, to garnish
- Lime wedge, to garnish

Method

Add all the ingredients, except for the garnish, to the cocktail shaker filled with ice.

Shake well until chilled and combined.

Strain into an ice-filled glass.

Garnish with fresh raspberries and lime wedge.

LAVENDER LURE

Lose yourself in a sweet, secret tryst among wildflowers. The delicate kiss of violet and citrus entwine in an intoxicating, fragrant dance that lures you into a moment of irresistible, fleeting indulgence, and lingers long after the scent has gone.

Ingredients

- 30 ml (1 fl oz) crème de violette
- 30 ml (1 fl oz) lemon cream liqueur

Method

Add the crème de violette to the shooter glass.

Using a bar spoon, carefully pour over the lemon cream liqueur.

Rust and Gold

A drink of quiet contrasts, blending the rugged warmth of toil and fight with a golden heart of unexpected luxury. Its deep brown hue speaks of hard-earned strength, while each mouthful reveals an irresistible elegance. Both intertwine in a dance of simplicity and grace.

Ingredients

- 2 dashes Angostura bitters
- Sugar cube
- 60 ml (2 fl oz) bourbon
- Ice cubes
- Soda water, to top
- Orange slice, to garnish

Method

Muddle together bitters and sugar cube in the bottom of the glass.

Add bourbon and stir, then add ice.

Top with soda water and garnish with orange slice.

Explore the wild possibilities of a stroll in the dark, where the moon is your only witness. Perfect for those with secrets to whisper and promises to make, who know that the night is brief and who see the sparkle of each precious moment.

Ingredients

- ½ tbsp runny honey
- ½ tbsp slightly cooled, boiled water
- 60 ml (2 fl oz) white rum
- 40 ml (1⅓ fl oz) lemon juice
- Ice cubes, for shaker, and for glass (optional)
- Twist of lemon, to garnish

Method

Add the honey and slightly cooled boiled water to the cocktail shaker (don't add ice yet) and stir until the honey has dissolved.

Add the rum to the honey and stir.

Add lemon juice and ice to the cocktail shaker and shake until combined and chilled.

Strain into the martini glass, over ice if you prefer it extra cold.

Serve with a twist of lemon.

Ruler of the Summer Court

A wondrously regal elixir – with its own fruit crown – that captures the allure of bountiful royalty across the land and summer gardens full of rampant growth. Feeling a little bit fruity?

Ingredients

- 200 g (7 oz) frozen watermelon, cubed
- 30 ml (1 fl oz) silver tequila
- 20 ml (⅔ fl oz) triple sec
- 1 tbsp caster sugar
- Juice of ½ lime
- Sparkling water, to top
- Watermelon wedge, to garnish

Method

In a blender, blitz the frozen watermelon, tequila, triple sec, sugar and lime juice.

Strain the mixture into a margarita glass.

Gently top with sparkling water and garnish with wedge of watermelon.

Velvet Comfort

From dragon slayers to devious nobles, we all need the respite of resting from time to time before rejoining the fray. Relish a velvety smooth embrace – perfect for time off from intrigue and passion.

Ingredients

- 60 ml (2 fl oz) dry vermouth
- 60 ml (2 fl oz) cognac
- 45 ml (1½ fl oz) apricot brandy
- 3 dashes Angostura bitters
- Ice cubes

Method

Add all the ingredients to a cocktail shaker.

Shake until fully combined and chilled.

Strain into a martini glass.

Rust-heart Phoenix

Witness the rise of the phoenix from the depths of mystery, its fiery beauty mirrored in every sip. An infusion that echoes the captivating allure of enchanted forests and autumn's embrace, it shimmers with a deep, earthy warmth, drawing you in like the mythical creature whose essence it holds.

Ingredients

- 15 ml (½ fl oz) tequila
- 15 ml (½ fl oz) vodka
- 15 ml (½ fl oz) triple sec
- 15 ml (½ fl oz) gin
- 15 ml (½ fl oz) rum
- 15 ml (½ fl oz) lemon or lime juice
- 20 ml (⅔ fl oz) simple syrup
- Ice cubes
- Cola, to top
- Lime slices, to garnish

Method

Add all the ingredients, except the cola and lime, into an ice-filled jug and stir with a bar spoon until fully mixed.

Add the cola to the jug and gently stir with bar spoon.

Pour into the glass. Garnish with lime slices.

Gilded Eden

Bask in the luminous splendour of a secret fruit garden, where golden hues kiss almond trees and all your secrets are safe. This elixir invites barefoot lovers and wanderers to dream up plot twists under ancient trees, where every sip feels like a taste of paradise.

Ingredients

- 30 ml (1 fl oz) white rum
- 30 ml (1 fl oz) dark rum
- 20 ml (⅔ fl oz) orange curaçao
- 15 ml (½ fl oz) almond syrup
- 30 ml (1 fl oz) lime juice
- 50 ml (1⅔ fl oz) pineapple juice
- Ice cubes, for shaker and glass
- Maraschino cherry and a segment of pineapple, to garnish

Method

Add all the ingredients, except the garnish, to a cocktail shaker.

Shake well until combined and chilled.

Strain cocktail into an ice-filled glass and top with pineapple and cherry.

Lemon Fae Delight

This luminous potion bursts with zesty brightness and a seductive sweetness, evoking sunshine and desire.

Ingredients

- 250 ml (8½ fl oz) water
- 200 g (7 oz) white caster sugar
- 275 ml (9⅓ fl oz) lemon juice
- 275 ml (9⅓ fl oz) lime juice
- 50 ml (1⅔ fl oz) tequila
- Ice cubes
- Salt, to garnish
- Lime, to rub on rim of glass (optional)
- Lime slice, to garnish

Method

To make the syrup, slowly heat the water and sugar in a saucepan, stirring until sugar is dissolved and the mix appears slightly thicker. Take off the heat and stir in the lemon and lime juice. Leave to cool.

While waiting for the lemon and lime syrup to cool, cover a plate with salt. Dip the rim of the glass in water, or rub with a lime, and roll the wet rim in the salt. Leave to dry.

Add 100 ml of the lemon and lime syrup and the tequila to an ice-filled cocktail shaker and shake until combined and cooled.

Strain into glass and garnish with lime slice.

DREAMSPINNER

Step into a world of tantalizing possibility with this clear elixir so pure it leaves no barriers between you and your desires. This seductive drink is said to weave fantasies into reality, inviting you to peer deeply, sip slowly and let your wildest dreams come to life.

Ingredients

- 60 ml (2 fl oz) gin
- 15 ml (½ fl oz) dry vermouth
- Ice cubes
- Olives, pitted and skewered on cocktail stick, to garnish

Method

Combine the gin and vermouth in a cocktail shaker with a handful of ice and shake to combine.

Strain into martini glass.

OR

Stir the gin and vermouth together in a chilled martini glass.

Garnish with olives.

The Weathered Sage

A drink that's perfect for the worldly-wise, and those who know a thing or two. Quietly powerful, not afraid of life's lessons and laced with a delicious herbal bitterness, this speaks of storms endured, heartache experienced and wisdom earned. Perfect for the end of the night, when truth-sayers gather.

Ingredients

- 30 ml (1 fl oz) bourbon
- 30 ml (1 fl oz) fernet liqueur
- 30 ml (1 fl oz) lemon juice
- Ice cubes, for shaker and glass
- Sprig of mint, to garnish

Method

Add all of the ingredients, except for the garnish, to a cocktail shaker.

Shake until fully combined and chilled.

Strain into an ice-filled old-fashioned glass.

Lightly bruise mint leaves and place on top as a garnish.

The Dancing Jester

Sweetly cheeky, full-bodied and full of charm, this cocktail twirls onto the scene with a wink and a grin. Smooth yet playful, it's the life of the party, ready to sweep you off your feet and keep you spinning till dawn. Made for sweet-talking jesters whose merry ways seduce and delight.

Ingredients

- 60 ml (2 fl oz) bourbon
- 10 mint leaves, plus a sprig to garnish
- 15 ml (½ fl oz) simple syrup
- Ice cubes, for shaker and glass

Method

Add the bourbon, mint, simple syrup and ice to a cocktail shaker and shake until combined and cooled.

Strain into glass, over ice.

Add sprig of mint to garnish.

Scented Temptress

The drink of choice for the charming seductress – bold, daring and always in control. With its irresistible sweetness and saucy undertones, it flirts with your senses and leaves a trail of desire in its wake. Perfect for weaving a love spell – or just having a wonderful time.

Ingredients

- 60 ml (2 fl oz) vodka
- 30 ml (1 fl oz) sake
- 60 ml (2 fl oz) lychee juice
- Ice cubes, for shaker and glass

Method

Add the vodka, sake, lychee juice and ice to the cocktail shaker and shake until combined.

Strain into an ice-filled glass.

Frosted Fruit Fable

Feel the burn of ice and fire, where tropical sweetness meets a frosty edge – and you'll be dazzled by the inevitable spark of opposites attracting. Like glancing at sparkling, pristine snow – and sensing the flaming burn within.

Ingredients

- 60 ml (2 fl oz) coconut cream
- 60 ml (2 fl oz) pineapple juice
- 60 ml (2 fl oz) white rum
- Pineapple slice, rind cut off
- Handful of ice
- Pineapple wedge and/or maraschino cherry, to garnish

Method

Blitz all the ingredients except the garnish in a blender on the highest speed until completely blended.

Pour into hurricane glass and garnish with wedge of pineapple and/or maraschino cherry.

Tainted Halo

Savour the duality of light and shadow, bitter and sweet, of a character whose good intentions come with a reminder of temptation just around the corner. Will you be good, or will you be bad?

Ingredients

- 25 ml (⅘ fl oz) gin
- 25 ml (⅘ fl oz) sweet vermouth
- 25 ml (⅘ fl oz) Campari
- Ice cubes, for shaker
- 1–2 oversized ice cubes, for glass
- Orange peel, to garnish

Method

Stir liquid ingredients together in an ice-filled cocktail shaker until combined and chilled.

Place the oversized ice cube(s) in the old-fashioned glass.

Strain the cocktail into the glass.

Garnish with orange peel.

Wrap yourself in the seductive cocoon of mystery and desire, a smooth creamy blend that lingers like a promise whispered in your ear. Each delicious mouthful is a quiet, tantalizing secret, a soft caress that hints at something more – once the others have disappeared.

Ingredients

- 30 ml (1 fl oz) crème de menthe
- 30 ml (1 fl oz) crème de cacao
- 40 ml (1⅓ fl oz) double cream
- Ice cubes
- Sprig of mint, to garnish

Method

Combine all liquid ingredients in cocktail shaker with ice.

Shake vigorously – the cream is thick so will need a little extra work to combine.

Strain into martini glass and garnish with mint.

Bittersweet Bliss

Even sunrises have a melancholy shadow behind them – and in this case, the brightest star is steeped and made in darkness. Celebrate the chemistry of opposites attracting, flickering with alchemy.

Ingredients

- 450 g (1 lb) oranges, sliced into wedges
- 250 g (9 oz) caster sugar
- 250 ml (8½ fl oz) cider vinegar
- Zest and juice of 1 orange
- 60 ml (2 fl oz) orange liqueur
- Ice cubes
- Orange slices, to garnish

Method

Muddle together orange wedges and half of the sugar in a large jar, seal and store in fridge for 4 hours.

Add remaining sugar and cider vinegar. Seal and shake and store overnight in cool, dark place.

Strain into fresh jar and stir in zest, juice and orange liqueur.

Pour into highball glasses filled with ice and garnish with orange slices.

New Beginnings

Surrender to the irresistible charm of sweet temptation, with a crisp, tangy twist that feels like opening the first page of a brand new romantasy novel. Each sip invites you into a world of thrilling possibilities, as intoxicating as the start of your next great adventure – whether that's in print, or in person.

Ingredients

- 1 lime, halved
- 4 mint leaves, plus a sprig to garnish
- 1 tsp granulated sugar
- 60 ml (2 fl oz) white rum
- Soda water, to top
- Ice cubes
- Lime wheels, to garnish

Method

Remove pips from the lime and squeeze the juice over the mint leaves and sugar in a cocktail shaker (without ice).

Muddle until the mint leaves are bruised.

Strain the mixture into an ice-filled glass.

Pour in the rum and gently stir together.

Top with soda water. Garnish with lime and mint.

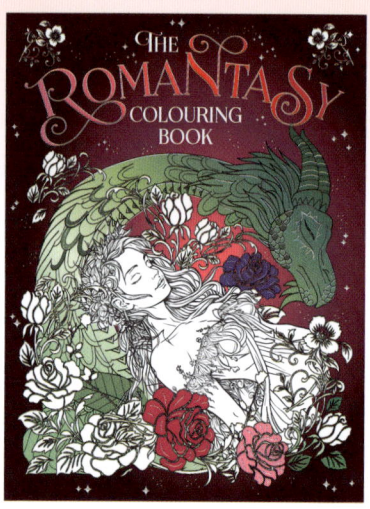

The Romantasy Colouring Book

Paperback | 978-1-83799-604-9

Step into the world of romantasy and bring this stunning collection of images to life with colour. Unleash your passion for romance and fantasy as you embark on your own artistic adventure. As you colour, you'll also read quotes to set your heart ablaze from the greatest and most loved romantasy novels.

The Romantasy Puzzle Book

Francis Nightingale

Hardback | 978-1-83799-684-1

Embark on a quest through the realm where romance and fantasy collide to solve the puzzles in this enchanting activity book. Inside these pages you'll discover classic conundrums and light-hearted games designed to immerse you in the world of romantasy. You're the main character of this story: it's up to you to solve away and save the day!

Have you enjoyed this book?
If so, find us on Facebook at **Summersdale Publishers**,
on Twitter/X at **@Summersdale** and on Instagram and
TikTok at **@summersdalebooks** and get in touch.
We'd love to hear from you!

www.summersdale.com

IMAGE CREDITS

Foliage throughout © Anton Dzyna/Shutterstock.com;
Roses throughout © tbs graphics/Shutterstock.com